The Room
in My
Heart

Presented to

_____

With Love From

_____

Date

_____

THE ROOM IN MY HEART
A Story for Expectant Children and Their Mommies

Published by Loyal Kids

A Division of Loyal Publishing Inc.

P.O. Box 1892, Sisters, OR 97759

www.loyalpublishing.com

Printed in Italy

International Standard Book Number: 1-929125-04-6

00   01   02   03   04   05   06 — 10   9   8   7   6   5   4   3   2   1

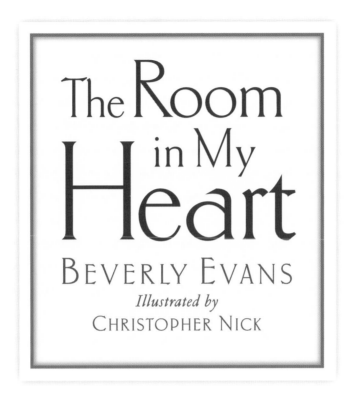

The Room in My Heart

BEVERLY EVANS

Illustrated by

CHRISTOPHER NICK

A Story for Expectant Children and Their Mommies

LOYAL KIDS

SISTERS, OREGON

There is a special place in my heart. It's a room.
A special room in my heart. It is just for you.

Long before you were born, my heart was very small.
But when Jesus came to live there, He began to make it bigger.
He began to build special rooms in my heart…
because He loves me!

First, Jesus built a special room in my heart for Daddy.
It is lit up with his smile. It is filled with
the music of his voice when he is happy or sad.

This special room is filled with my love for him!

After Daddy's room was finished and complete,
Jesus began building another special room in my heart.
Your room! Just for you. It is lit up with your smile.
It is filled with the music you make as you play.

It is filled with my love for YOU!

When your room was ready, you were born!
I had never had a room in my heart like yours before.
Now Jesus is building another room in my heart -
Baby's room! It will be lit up with baby's smile.
It will be filled with the music of baby's voice.

It will be filled with my love for Baby.

When Baby's room is ready, Baby will be born!
I've never had a room just like Baby's before.
It will look just like Baby.

Baby's room will never take the place of your room.
Your room holds the special love I have for you.
And Baby's room holds the special love I have for Baby.

Just like my tummy has grown bigger,
my heart has grown bigger, too.
After Baby is born, my tummy will grow smaller again.
But not my heart.

My heart will stay big, with its rooms for
Daddy, and Baby, and YOU!

In our house, we must share things.

You share your toys.
You share your room and your closet.

You share your mommy's lap.
But you never have to share
your special room in my heart.
It is yours alone.
It is there, just for you!

In our house, you must help to keep your room clean.
But you do not clean your special room in my heart.

Jesus keeps it clean for me!
When I am angry, or lose my temper,
or forget to be the best Mommy to you,
Jesus comes to me and whispers...

"There's a mess in that room.
Come on! Let's clean it up together."

And then I can forgive…or ask for forgiveness…
or do whatever it takes to make things right!
Even when that room gets messy,
it is still your special room.
It is filled with my love for you.

One day, you will be a grown up like me.

You will have your own children.

You will have your own home.

You will have rooms in your heart.

But you will never leave that special room in my heart.

It will always be your special room.

There's a special place in my heart. It's a room!!

It's a special room in my heart.

It's a special room in my heart
just for you!